Discard

# Totally WACKY FACTS ABOUT EXPLORING SPACE

## EMMA CARLSON BERNE

CAPSTONE PRESS
a capstone imprint

A huge air hockey-like floor helps astronauts learn to move heavy objects in space.

Astronauts train for space walks in a giant SWIMMING POOL.

WANT TO BE AN ASTRONAUT? FIRST YOU HAVE TO LOG 1,000 HOURS FLYING JETS!

What does it
feel like to
float in space?
Try riding NASA's
VOMIT COMET!

It flies to 34,000 feet (10,363 meters), then nosedives to 10,000 feet (3,048 m).

5

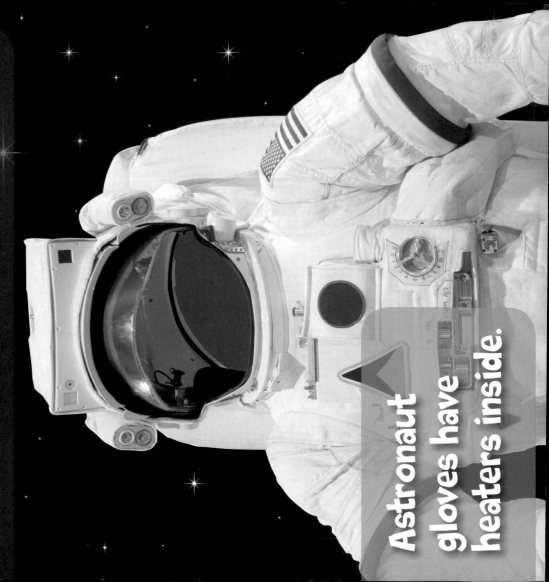

You can live for about 30 seconds in outer space without a space suit of any kind.

Astronaut gloves have heaters inside.

Space suit pants have handles to help pull them on.

On Earth a space suit weighs 280 pounds (127 kilograms) and takes 45 minutes to put on.

Heart muscles can weaken after more than seven days in space.

Long spaceflights give astronauts blurry vision.

8

SPACE CAN MAKE YOUR HEAD **SWELL!**

While orbiting Earth, astronauts see a sunset or sunrise every 45 MINUTES.

Some say space smells like meat and metals. Others say it smells like raspberries!

Got **dirty underwear,** astronaut? Just send it into space, where it burns up in **EARTH'S ATMOSPHERE!**

Astronauts wear special cooling underwear.

If an astronaut pukes in space, it floats in LITTLE GLOBS!

Astronauts wear adult diapers!

DURING AN EARLY MISSION, AN ASTRONAUT HAD TO WEAR RUBBER PANTS TO POOP IN.

Pants that draw blood to the legs make an astronaut's heart work HARDER IN SPACE.

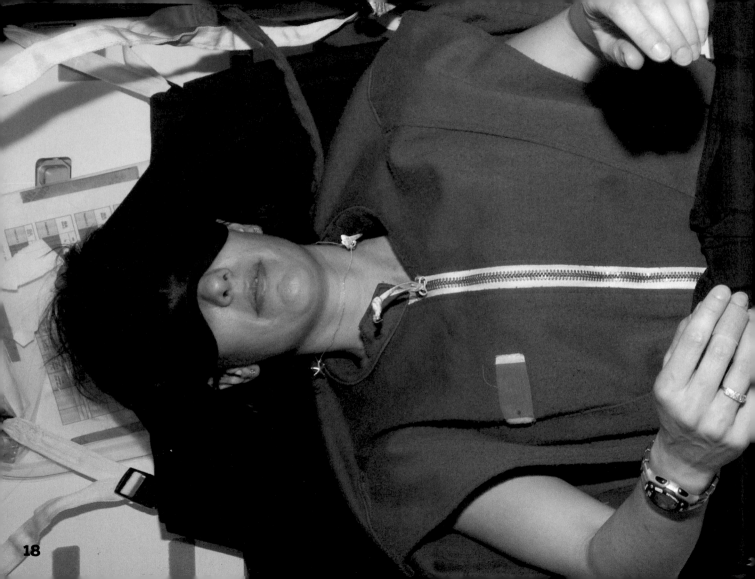

An astronaut straps herself down with **VELCRO** to keep from floating around during sleep.

**DURING A ROCKET LAUNCH, G-FORCES MAKE YOUR BODY FEEL FOUR TIMES HEAVIER.**

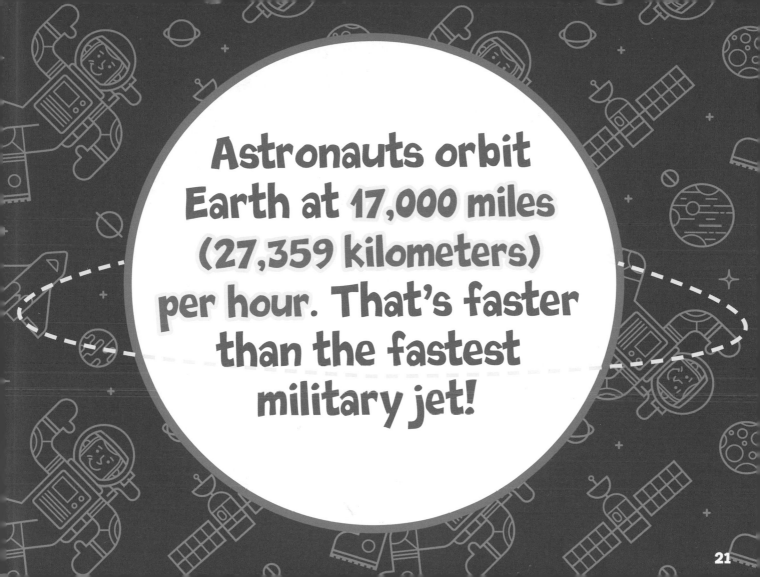

Astronauts orbit Earth at 17,000 miles (27,359 kilometers) per hour. That's faster than the fastest military jet!

Weightlessness in space allows an astronaut to lift really heavy things.

# MISSION CONTROL

SOMETIMES WAKES UP ASTRONAUTS BY BLASTING THEIR FAVORITE SONGS.

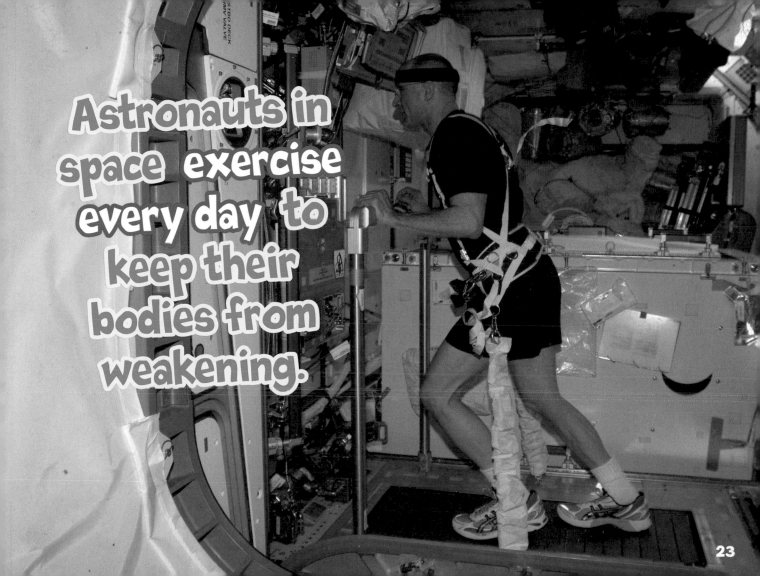

Astronauts in space exercise every day to keep their bodies from weakening.

ASTRONAUTS USED TO EAT FOOD FROM TOOTHPASTE-LIKE TUBES.

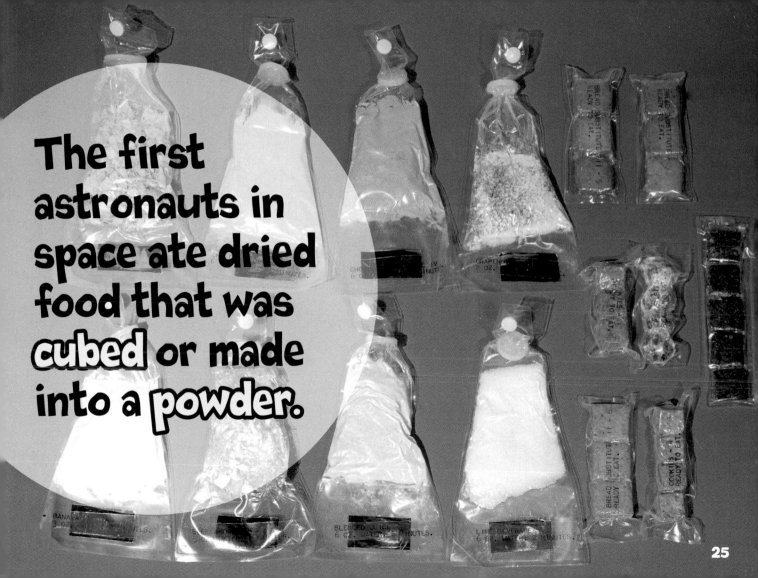

The first astronauts in space ate dried food that was **cubed** or made into a **powder**.

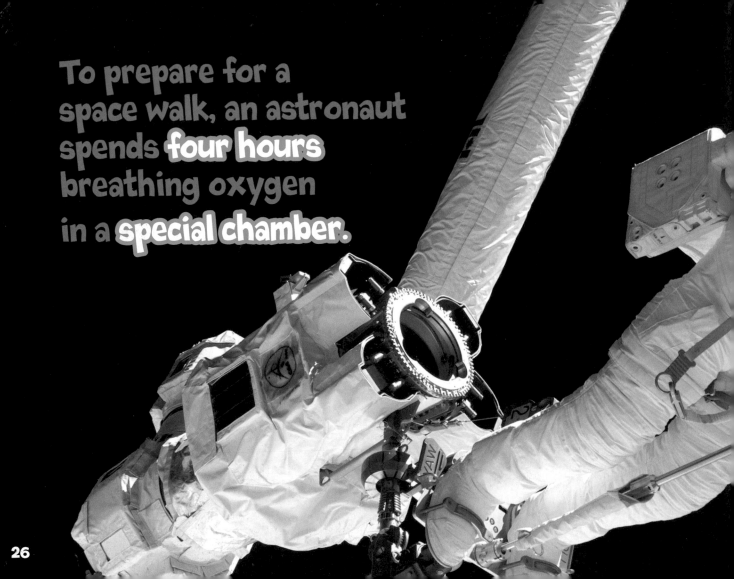

To prepare for a space walk, an astronaut spends **four hours** breathing oxygen in a **special chamber.**

A **robotic arm** carries space-walking astronauts from place to place.

During a space walk the temperature outside can be as high as **250°F (121°C)** or as low as **-250°F (-157°C)**.

AFTER RETURNING FROM SPACE, AN ASTRONAUT MAY FALL OVER WHEN WALKING.

Astronauts who spend a lot of time in space can have **BONE LOSS.**

Today the International Space Station (ISS) is as large as a U.S. football field!

250 MILES (402 KM): THE DISTANCE FROM EARTH TO THE ISS

The first two parts of the **ISS** were launched into space in **1998.**

Astronauts have an oven and a toaster onboard the ISS, but no refrigerator or microwave.

THE ISS HAS TWO BATHROOMS AND A GYM.

A six-bedroom house has as much living space as the ISS.

IN SPACE, SODA POP BUBBLES SEPARATE FROM THE SODA.

Astronauts use liquid salt because floating salt crystals could get stuck in vents.

Toilets in space work like giant vacuum cleaners.

ON THE ISS PEE IS PURIFIED AND TURNED INTO DRINKING WATER.

On the ISS astronauts wash their hair with a pouch of hot water and rinseless shampoo.

ASTRONAUTS IN SPACE
CLEAN THEMSELVES WITH
WIPES AND TOWELS.

Dogs, mice, rabbits, turtles, jellyfish, insects, spiders, and fish have all traveled into SPACE.

**MORE THAN 2,000 ANIMALS WENT ON ONE SPACE MISSION IN 1998.**

In 1957 a Russian dog named Laika was the first live being to orbit EARTH.

43

A satellite has to zoom along at about **17,500 miles (28,164 km) per hour** to stay in orbit.

The Soviet Union launched the first artificial satellite, *Sputnik 1*, in 1957. It was the size of a BEACH BALL.

A Russian named Yuri Gagarin was the first human to orbit Earth in 1961.

About one month later, Alan Shepard Jr. became the first American in space.

IN 1968 THE EUROPEAN SPACE RESEARCH ORGANIZATION LAUNCHED THE FIRST EUROPEAN SATELLITE INTO SPACE.

In 1962 John Glenn sped around Earth three times. He was the first American to ORBIT EARTH.

ON GLENN'S RETURN TO EARTH, HIS SPACE CAPSULE NEARLY BURNED UP.

Astronaut John Glenn was 77 years old during his last space mission.

SCIENTISTS ONCE THOUGHT MOON DUST WOULD SWALLOW A SPACECRAFT TRYING TO LAND ON THE MOON.

THE *RANGER* SPACECRAFT WERE DESIGNED TO ZOOM TOWARD THE MOON, TAKE A BUNCH OF PICTURES, AND THEN CRASH.

The Apollo 11 astronauts practiced moon walking at the GRAND CANYON.

NEIL ARMSTRONG

— MICHAEL COLLINS

BUZZ ALDRIN

ON JULY 20, 1969, APOLLO 11 ASTRONAUTS NEIL ARMSTRONG AND BUZZ ALDRIN LANDED ON THE MOON.

52

# THE APOLLO 11 ASTRONAUTS TRAVELED 240,000 MILES (386,243 KM) IN 76 HOURS.

Traveling across England by horse and carriage takes longer than **flying to the moon.**

If this horse doesn't turn around, this trip could take **FOREVER!**

When Armstrong and Aldrin landed on the moon, they had only **20–40 seconds** of fuel left in the lunar module.

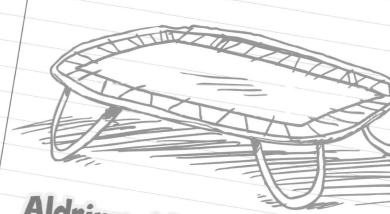

Aldrin said walking on the moon was like walking on a trampoline, without bounciness.

THE APOLLO 11 ASTRONAUTS SAVED THEIR LIVES WITH A **PEN** WHEN A SPACECRAFT SWITCH BROKE OFF.

An American flag that Armstrong and Aldrin had planted on the moon fell over as the lunar module blasted off.

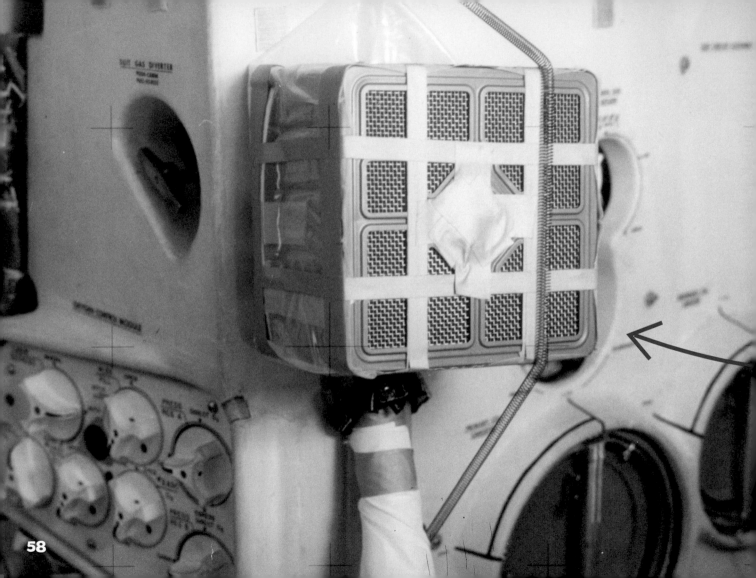

IN AN EMERGENCY APOLLO 13 ASTRONAUTS MADE CARBON DIOXIDE FILTERS OUT OF CARDBOARD, PLASTIC BAGS, AND DUCT TAPE.

Astronaut Alan Shepard Jr. played GOLF on the MOON.

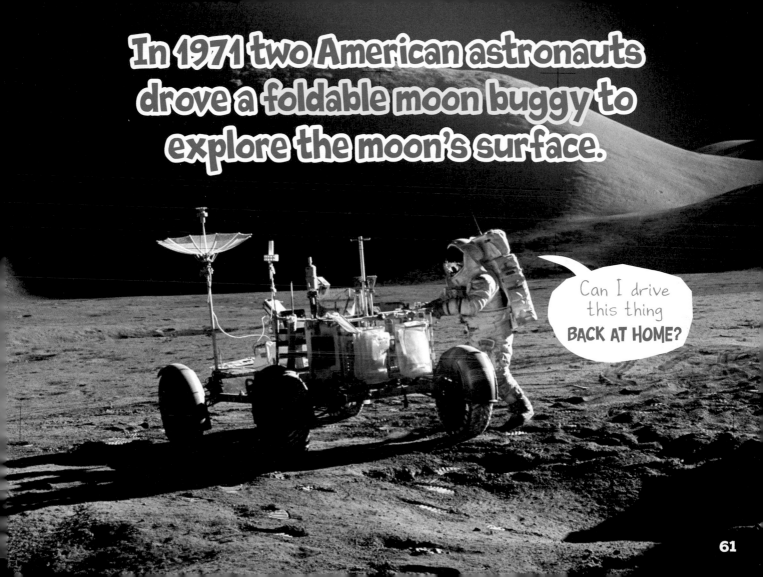

The first U.S. space station, *Skylab*, orbited Earth from 1973 to 1979.

**Skylab was about as long as a 6-story building!**

In 1979 *Skylab* crashed into the Indian Ocean, and some parts fell onto land in Western Australia.

In 1977 the United States launched twin spacecraft, *Voyager 1 and Voyager 2*, into space.

TITAN/CENTAUR

BOTH *VOYAGER 1* AND *VOYAGER 2* TAKE PICTURES SHARP ENOUGH TO READ A NEWSPAPER HEADLINE FROM ½ MILE (0.8 KM) AWAY.

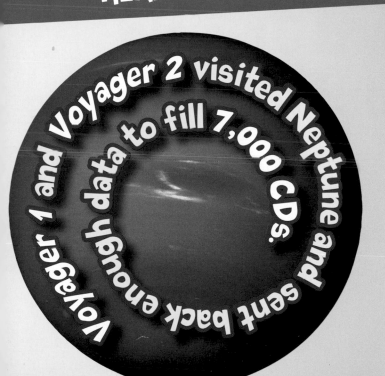

Voyager 1 and Voyager 2 visited Neptune and sent back enough data to fill 7,000 CDs.

*VOYAGER 1* has traveled farther from Earth than any other spacecraft.

Just before blasting off into space, astronaut Alan Shepard Jr. told Mission Control that he had to PEE.

In 1980 a European company called Arianespace became the first commercial space transport company.

In 1981 the first U.S. space shuttle, Columbia, launched from Kennedy Space Center, in Florida.

Columbia weighed 178,000 pounds (80,739 kg)—as much as 13 elephants!

THE SHUTTLE'S HEAT SHIELD WAS BUILT USING MORE THAN 30,000 TILES MADE OF SAND.

The space shuttle *Discovery* put on enough miles to go to the moon and back 300 times!

In 1963 Valentina Tereshkova from Russia became the first woman in space.

EILEEN COLLINS BECAME THE FIRST WOMAN TO PILOT A SPACECRAFT WHEN SHE PILOTED THE *DISCOVERY* IN 1995.

NASA retired the space shuttles in 2011, after 30 years of service.

About 400 TREES had to be cut down so the shuttle *Endeavour* could fit through the streets on its trip to the museum.

ENDEAVOUR WAS FLOWN ON TOP OF A JETLINER WHEN IT WENT TO A MUSEUM.

The Hubble Space Telescope is as long as a

LARGE SCHOOL BUS.

STOP

BUS NO. 99

HUBBLE WEIGHS AS MUCH AS TWO ELEPHANTS.

Every hour and a half, Hubble makes one trip around Earth.

HUBBLE CAN SEE GALAXIES THAT ARE BILLIONS OF LIGHT-YEARS AWAY.

Hubble can see comet pieces crash into the **atmosphere** above **Jupiter.**

**The Hubble Telescope** helped discover dark matter—strange energy that helps the

# UNIVERSE EXPAND.

HUBBLE IS THE ONLY TELESCOPE EVER DESIGNED TO BE REPAIRED IN SPACE.

Hubble can see better than ground telescopes, because Earth's atmosphere isn't in the way.

SUNLIGHT POWERS THE HUBBLE TELESCOPE.

THE JAMES WEBB SPACE TELESCOPE (JWST) IS THE NEXT HUBBLE—AND A SORT OF TIME MACHINE.

JWST WILL BE ABLE TO SEE THE FIRST STARS FROM THE BEGINNING OF THE UNIVERSE.

JWST can see the writing on a penny 24 miles (39 km) away.

The JWST can fold up to fit inside a rocket only 16 feet (5 m) wide.

JWST HAS INSTRUMENTS THAT ARE KEPT COLDER THAN -370°F (-223°C) IN ORDER TO OPERATE.

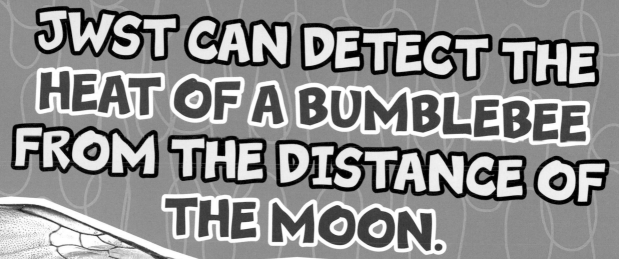

# JWST CAN DETECT THE HEAT OF A BUMBLEBEE FROM THE DISTANCE OF THE MOON.

IN 2014 THE EUROPEAN SPACE AGENCY (ESA) SPACECRAFT

ROSETTA

RELEASED A SMALL PROBE THAT LANDED ON A COMET.

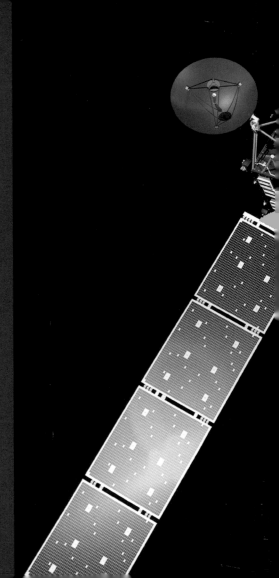

Scientists are tracking **500,000 pieces** of space junk orbiting Earth right now.

SPACE JUNK MOVES AT 17,500 MILES (28,164 KM) PER HOUR AND CAN ACT LIKE BULLETS.

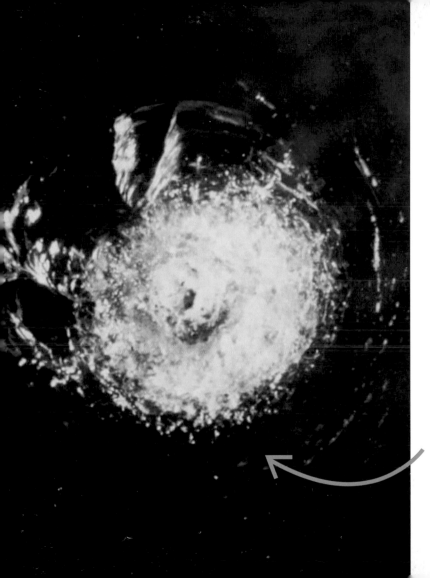

# PAINT FLECKS

can move so fast in orbit, that they have cracked spacecraft windows.

91

SCIENTISTS ARE STUDYING HOW TO MAKE AN ION ELECTRIC "GUN" TO FIRE ROCKETS INTO SPACE.

Sail-like mirrors that capture sunlight may one day power spacecraft.

NASA's goal is to send astronauts to land on an **ASTEROID** by 2025.

Astronauts could explore the asteroid to practice for a Mars landing.

THE ROVERS SPIRIT AND OPPORTUNITY HAVE EXPLORED SEVERAL MILES OF MARS.

THE ROVERS WERE SUPPOSED TO RUN FOR ONLY 90 DAYS.

SPIRIT OPERATED FOR 6 YEARS, AND OPPORTUNITY IS STILL RUNNING 10 YEARS LATER.

The Mars rover Curiosity is about as tall as a basketball player.

CURIOSITY HAS A HEAD, ARMS, and LEGS.

*Curiosity* can take pictures of objects smaller than the width of a human hair.

Curiosity takes SELFIES.

IN 2005 THE ESA PROBE *HUYGENS* LANDED ON **SATURN'S MOON TITAN.** NO OTHER SPACECRAFT LAUNCHED FROM **EARTH** HAS LANDED FARTHER AWAY.

In the 19th century, people saw canals on Mars with telescopes.

IN 1965 WE GOT THE FIRST CLOSE LOOK AT MARS FROM A SMALL SPACECRAFT FLYBY.

The first
spacecraft on
Mars took pictures
for **20 seconds**
before it went
**DARK.**

Astronaut Umberto Guidoni became the first European to visit the ISS in 2001.

IN 2001
DENNIS TITO
PAID $20 MILLION
TO RUSSIAN
SPACE OFFICIALS
FOR A 10-DAY
TRIP TO SPACE!

WANT TO TAKE A RIDE TO SPACE?

For $250,000 you can sign up for a future seat on a Virgin Galactic spacecraft.

CAN YOU

At almost 438 days, Russian Valeri Polyakov holds the record for the most consecutive days in space.

# BEAT THIS?

## THE LONGEST SPACE WALK LASTED 8 HOURS AND 56 MINUTES!

The fastest human spaceflight flew at 24,791 miles (39,897 km) per hour!

# GLOSSARY

**artificial**—made by people

**asteroid**—a small rocky object that orbits the sun

**atmosphere**—the layer of gases that surrounds some planets, dwarf planets, and moons

**carbon dioxide**—an odorless, colorless gas made of carbon and oxygen atoms

**comet**—a ball of rock and ice that circles the Sun

**commercial**—to do with buying and selling things

**g-force**—the force of gravity on a moving object

**galaxy**—a large group of stars and planets

**International Space Station (ISS)**—a place for astronauts to live and work in space

**ion**—an atom that has an electrical charge

**lunar module**—a moon vehicle

**orbit**—to travel around an object in space; an orbit is also the path an object follows while circling an object in space

**satellite**—an object, either natural or man-made that orbits a planet

**transport**—to move something from one place to another

# READ MORE

Pastan, Amy. *The Smithsonian Book of Air & Space* Trivia. Washington, D.C.: Smithsonian Books, 2014.

*Ripley's Believe It or Not Kids Fun Facts and Silly Stories the Big One!* Orlando, Fla.: Ripley Pub., 2014.

Shereda, Laura. *Spectacular Space Trivia*. Ultimate Trivia Challenge. New York: Gareth Stevens Pub., 2014.

# INTERNET SITES

FactHound offers a safe, fun way to find Internet sites related to this book. All of the sites on FactHound have been researched by our staff.

Here's all you do:

Visit *www.facthound.com*

Type in this code: 9781491465240